M000076464

VIRGO
August 23–September 22

Crystal Astrology for Modern Life

SANDY SITRON

CONTENTS

CRYSTALS, ASTROLOGY AND YOU

UNDERSTANDING VIRGO

VIRGO
THROUGHOUT
THE YEAR

LUNAR
ENERGY AND
MERCURY IN MOTION

CRYSTALS, ASTROLOGY AND YOU

THE STONES,
THE SIGNS AND YOU

The stars above you and the stones beneath your feet are part of the fabric of your world. Astrology offers a cosmic perspective. Crystals radiate with the healing energy of the Earth. Together, they serve as guides in your life, engaged in a vibrational conversation that can help you reflect on, and tune into, who you are. Birthstones and other crystals can be used to highlight and harness the energy of your astrological birth chart.

As above, so below – harness the power of crystals and the cosmos to create a deeper connection with yourself for a confident, empowered, high-vibe life.

Astrology is the ancient study of the changing positions and alternating energy of the celestial bodies and how this relates to our lives on Earth. The unique cosmic environment that you synced up with at the moment of your first breath provides awareness of – and offers a way to interpret – your personality traits, core strengths, growth areas, emotional style and so much more. When you better understand your vibrational self, it's easier to make informed choices about the big and small things in your life. Your conscious perspective is uplifted. Your mind is opened and activated.

Crystals, or 'stones', vibrate with the breath of the Earth. They act on an energetic level, sending vibrations out into the world. They are natural amplifiers of positive energy and bring discordant energies into balance. Each crystal has its own energy blueprint, which is why different types of stones may influence the human energy field in different ways. Pairing the insight that you gain from astrology with the healing power of crystals can help you navigate certain life areas and facilitate personal transformation and spiritual growth throughout the astrological year.

Crystals and the constellations call to us. In this book you'll receive a bespoke selection of crystals to help you amplify or balance the unique energies of your sign. You'll gain insight into your life, activate your highest potential and learn to live harmoniously with the energy that surrounds you.

When gazing at the night sky, when you hold a crystal in your hand, feel inspired to slow down, be present in the moment and get ready to embark on a meaningful journey of self-discovery.

YOUR UNIQUE RECOMMENDATIONS

We all accept that different things work for different people. Advice that's a perfect fit for one person might fall flat for someone else. Regardless of where Virgo sits in your personal astrology, this book will help you understand your Virgo nature and give you specific crystal recommendations for your sign and each astrological season. You can use these bespoke Virgo crystals to build confidence, spark creativity, feel more present, harmonize relationships, attract love, embrace your emotions, cultivate friendships, create abundance, optimize your health and wellness, amplify your natural gifts and find balance.

YOUR ASTRO-CRYSTAL JOURNEY

Once you understand how the two energetic studies of crystals and astrology relate to your life, you'll be ready to take a deep dive into your Virgo energy and learn to use crystals to leverage the strengths of your Virgo gifts, whether Virgo is your Sun, Moon or Rising sign, or elsewhere in your unique astrology. You'll also discover your unique Virgo crystal recommendations for love, friendship, money, work and health to help you connect to your true potential and reach your goals.

As each astrological season holds a different kind of energy, this book will take you through the year and show you how crystals can help you channel your unique Virgo energy under each sign. In this way, you will learn to navigate through the seasons with ease and to harmonize with the cycles of nature. You will discover how crystals can help you embrace the ebb and flow of the 29-day Moon cycle, enable you to sail through Mercury Retrograde and even plan your week.

This book is part of a series that unites each of the twelve zodiac signs with recommended crystals. When you are ready to go deeper on your astro-crystal journey, you may choose to purchase the companion books in the series that correspond to the other prominent signs in your birth chart.

THE
STONES

Dazzling gemstones are typically formed deep under the Earth's surface, stimulated by the combination of mineral-rich water, heat and pressure. Subterranean 'gardens' nurture the formation of billions of atoms into highly ordered, three-dimensional repeating patterns to create unique crystals, each one holding a vibrational record of earthly, physical reality.

Across the world and over millennia, people have been fascinated by crystals. Lucent jewels have captured the imagination for over 30,000 years. In the Democratic Republic of the Congo, small tools decorated with Quartz have been found that date back to 33,000 BCE. The Ancient Sumerians of Mesopotamia (present-day Iraq) used crystals for rituals and magic in the fourth century BCE. Humankind has used crystals for decoration, status, currency, religion, healing, magic-making and, in more recent times, modern technology. Early radios used crystals as electrical and tuning components. Today's computers, LCD screens and some batteries rely on crystal technology.

Good Vibrations People across different cultures and generations have turned to crystals as guides or helpers because it seems that, whatever facet of earthly experience you are struggling with, there is a crystal frequency that can help you move forwards on your path. Crystals may help bring calm and heal stress, empower you when you need support or confidence, or provide focus and clarity when you're struggling with an important decision. Crystals are thought to absorb the energy that you are trying to release and release the energy you are trying to absorb.

For example, if you are feeling dull and listless, Carnelian may share with you a vibration of high energy and drive. If you are overheated or stressed, Rose Quartz may help you soften and relax. Choosing the right crystal that resonates with, or reacts to, your energy can shift your mood or your mindset.

CHOOSING YOUR CRYSTALS

In Part Two of this book, you will be guided to a selection of crystals that are energetically aligned with your unique astrology. If you are adding these stones to your collection, it's important to choose responsibly.

Sustainability and Ethics   How did the crystal that you have in your hand make its way to you? The answer to this question is incredibly important to the well-being of humanity and the Earth.

The crystal industry is shrouded in mystery and plagued by bad practices. When you purchase a crystal, make sure to find gems that have a traceable, and short, journey from the mine to your hand. It's important to know if the mine that the crystal came from uses ethical, safe and sustainable practices. Discover if the lapidary, where the crystal was cut and polished, is a safe place that pays a living wage to the people who work there. The easiest way to do this is to mindfully source your crystals from sellers who have done the legwork. You vote with your financial choices. Make sure that you are contributing to better health and safety for all.

More information about sustainable and ethical practices and purveyors can be found on my website www.sandysitron.com/crystals.

Size, Finish and Price   When harnessing the power of a crystal for personal use, the size of the stone doesn't matter. If you are holding a crystal or carrying it close to your body, its vibration is in your energy field and will have an effect whatever its size.

A raw stone is a stone that is untreated. These are just as effective to use in healing practices as a crystal that has been tumbled or polished. So when you are choosing a crystal, choose one that appeals to you, no matter the size or finish.

The stones selected in this book can be sourced at an affordable price. Although some of the stones mentioned may sound ultra-luxurious and expensive, these crystals are available at a range of values.

YOUR CRYSTAL
TOOLKIT

In the next section, you'll find crystal
recommendations for your specific sign. First,
here are a few indispensable crystals to round out your
toolkit. These selections are a wonderful support for
anyone at any time.

GROUNDING AND PROTECTION

CLEANSING YOUR ENERGY

Smoky Quartz Getting grounded is the basis of spiritual work. So many factors in everyday life pull us out of ourselves. Spending too much time on your phone, not enough time in nature or eating too much sugar are common culprits, but the list goes on. If you want to nail your next meeting at work, remember where your keys are, or get on top of that to-do list, you need to get grounded. Feeling grounded also allows you to be present in your relationships and tuned in to your physical needs. This is where Smoky Quartz can help. This crystal keeps you centred, and emotionally clear. It may help you take a more practical view of a situation. On a more mystical level, Smoky Quartz has the effect of protecting you from energetic drains on your system. It is an excellent protection stone and just holding it can help you feel steady.

Selenite Just as you bathe your body regularly, it makes sense to regularly cleanse your energy system too. Energetic cleansing can help you balance your emotions and clear your mind. Cleanse your energy after work, socializing or spending time in a crowd. Or employ Selenite to help you get rid of emotional residue after a tough conversation. Energy cleansing is also recommended when you are going through any kind of transition – a break-up, a move or some other important milestone. Use Selenite with the intention of purifying your energy field and cleansing yourself of anything that is dragging you down. Imagine that it shines a ray of light through your entire body, clearing and cleansing.

Smoky Quartz Ritual	Selenite Ritual
Perform the grounding practice on page 26 while holding Smoky Quartz to anchor you.	Selenite can also be used to cleanse the energy of your other stones. Place a Selenite stone next to your crystals overnight.

SOOTHING RELAXATION

Rose Quartz   We all know what it's like to get stressed out and frazzled. Sometimes the nervous system is overloaded and it's hard to calm down. When that happens, you need a soothing crystal ally that can help you relax. If you are having trouble sleeping, are feeling on edge, or are working through some challenging emotions, it's time to soften with Rose Quartz. This dreamy pink stone is known for its inherent ability to calm and reassure. It soothes you while strengthening your capacity for empathy and compassion. If you're feeling down, lonely or heartbroken, let this crystalline stress-reliever support you.

FINDING YOUR DIRECTION

Clear Quartz   Clear quartz is a true all-purpose stone. When you actively set an intention with Clear Quartz, the stone will magnify that intention. When your world is changing around you and you need to forge ahead in a new direction, Clear Quartz will get you there. Clear Quartz can help you clarify, strategize and set your aspirations for your life. Once programmed with your wishes and desires, this powerful amplifier will hold the vibration of your intentions and help you visualize and realize your future.

Rose Quartz Ritual	Clear Quartz Ritual
Infuse a tumbled Rose Quartz stone in your next cup of tea or glass of water for a mindful moment with a soothing elixir.	Write an affirmation that inspires you. Say your affirmation aloud while holding Clear Quartz.

INTUITION
AND INSIGHT

Amethyst Your intuition is your
natural guidance system. It's that gut
feeling you have when something feels
wrong, or when something feels just
right. Intuition shows up in different
ways for everyone but it's like a muscle
that can be strengthened. If you have
questions about your life and you want
to tune into the answers, Amethyst
is at your service. In those moments,
practice asking and listening and let
this violet stone help open up your
mind's eye. Amethyst is also a fantastic
friend when you need help saying
the right thing in your next important
conversation, meeting or presentation.
Or if you are looking for a sparkling
boost to your creativity, open the
channels of inspiration with Amethyst
by your side.

	Amethyst Ritual	

The next time you have a question about your life or
path, lie down and place an Amethyst stone on your forehead or
near the crown of your head. Meditate and make space for
the answer to come through.

THE SIGNS

ASTROLOGY AND YOU

You are a unique being, made up of a solar system of characteristics that define your identity. Astrology illuminates your personality and your path. It describes how you think, learn, love, act and much more. Astrology can also be used to understand the energy of the moment.

Astrology has been contributed to by cultures throughout the world over thousands of years. The astrology used in this book is drawn from contemporary Western astrology. Like all things in the universe, the movements of the planets through the zodiac create a vibration. At the moment of your first breath, this energy is mirrored within you.

Your astrology is much more complex than just your star sign. The movements of the planets under the zodiac, in the exact place, at the exact moment you were born form your birth chart, a personalized map of the sky from your unique vantage point on Earth when you took your first breath. As well as showing you where the Sun lands in your chart, denoting your star sign, it also shows under which signs the Moon and other planets fall – this is the key to understanding your personal energetic code.

In order to discover your unique astrological make-up first you need to map your birth chart.

SUN, MOON AND RISING SIGN

When someone asks, 'What's your sign?' they are actually referring to your Sun sign, but it's worth learning your Moon and Rising signs too. These three symbols are a good place to begin your astrological journey as they represent the basic outline of who you are – like a simple sketch that captures your likeness in just a few brushstrokes. Together these three symbols make up your inner and outer self.

Casting Your Birth Chart Go to www.sandysitron.com/crystals and enter your birth data in the 'Create Your Birth Chart' tool. You'll then receive your birth chart, also called your natal chart, that shows the signs that the planets were in when you were born, and where they were located in the sky.

SUN
SIGN

· The Sun is a constant bright light, it symbolizes your ego, the part of you that you consciously identify with. It's how you tend to think of yourself.

· The Sun is the gravitational centre of the solar system, it represents your core self and describes your fundamental character and values.

· The Sun is the energy source that creates life on our planet, it signifies how you channel your energy.

MOON
SIGN

· The Moon is most visible at night, it symbolizes the part of you that is hard to see – your subconscious self.

· The Moon changes shape through the lunar month. It represents your ever-changing emotions and how you respond subconsciously to your feelings.

· The Moon is a satellite that circles the Earth, it describes how you turn inwards to protect, nurture and soothe yourself.

RISING
SIGN

· The Rising sign, also known as your Ascendant, is the constellation of the zodiac that was rising on the eastern horizon at the precise moment of your birth.

· The Rising sign shines new light into the world. It symbolizes how the rays of your personality beam out ahead as you walk down the street, meet new people, or interact on social media. It represents your vibe or your 'brand'. It epitomizes how other people see you.

· As you explore the following pages, you'll learn how to balance and enhance your unique energy using supportive crystals. Whatever your Sun, Moon or Rising sign, this book will help you find alignment and teach you how to leverage your inherent gifts.

PLANETS

SUN
☉

MOON
☽

MERCURY
☿

VENUS
♀

MARS
♂

JUPITER
♃

SATURN
♄

URANUS
♅

NEPTUNE
♆

PLUTO
♇

DEC 22–JAN 19 ♑

JAN 20–FEB 18 ♒

CAPRICORN

AQUARIUS

GARNET

AMETHYST

FEB 19–MAR 20 ♓

PISCES

AQUAMARINE

MAR 21–APR 19 ♈

ARIES

JASPER

EMERALD

APR 20–MAY 20 ♉

TAURUS

AGATE

GEMINI

MAY 21–JUN 21 ♊

DATES ARE APPROXIMATE AS THE DATES OF THE
SIGNS VARY BY ABOUT A DAY FROM YEAR TO YEAR.

ELEMENTS

FIRE
△

EARTH
▽

AIR
△

WATER
▽

NOV 22–DEC 21

OCT 24–NOV 21

SEP 23–OCT 23

AUG 23–SEP 22

JUL 23–AUG 22

JUN 22–JUL 22

SAGITTARIUS

SCORPIO

LIBRA

VIRGO

LEO

CANCER

RUBY

TOPAZ

OPAL

SAPPHIRE

CARNELIAN

MOONSTONE

MODALITY

CARDINAL
⋀

FIXED
□

MUTABLE
⌒

TOOLS FOR
YOUR JOURNEY

As you go forwards on your astro-crystal journey, two
key tools can help you gain insight and create positive
change – intuition and intention. Intuition helps you know
what you want and intention helps you make it happen.

LETTING YOUR
INTUITION GUIDE YOU

Everyone is intuitive, your intuition or 'inner
knowing' is your built-in guidance system. Use the
following prompts to strengthen your inner voice.

How to Connect
with Your Intuition

Slow down Take a few deep breaths and close your eyes. The more you can slow down in your life (even for just five minutes) the louder your intuitive voice grows.

Pose a question What do you want to know? Ask yourself. Say it aloud or ponder it silently. Or choose to write it down, sketch it or even dance it out. However you pose the question, make sure it is clear. If you aren't sure what to ask, try, 'what do I need to know that I don't yet know?'

Listen for the answer You might hear words or notice a sensation in your body. You might write down your question in a notebook then flip the page and write down the answer. You might have an emotional response or feel compelled to move in a certain way. Pay attention.

Practice The more you practice asking and listening, the more you get to understand your unique intuitive voice. Just as weightlifting tones your physical body, practicing these steps improves your intuitive muscle, so stick with it!

INTENTION
SETTING

In your meditations and rituals, you can program your crystals with the intentions or affirmations that will help you meet your goals.
An intention is a new thought that you would like to think. Our subconscious minds save energy by putting certain thoughts and habits on repeat. This survival skill has benefits, such as giving us more energy and space for other things, but it also has its downsides, such as getting us stuck in a negative pattern. One way to break in a new way of thinking is to intentionally repeat a new thought. Here is how to 'affirm' your new way of thinking into being!

Define what it is you would like to change.
Where are you feeling stuck? What is the pattern
that is bugging you? For example, 'I am stuck
because I have these exciting ideas for new
projects, but I never finish what I start.'

· <u>Decide what you want</u>
For instance, 'It would be great if I
finished my projects.'

· <u>Make it an 'I' statement</u>
Such as, 'I finish my projects.'

· <u>Make it affirmative</u>
Make sure your affirmation is
positively stated. Say what you want,
not what you don't want. So 'I finish
my projects' not 'I no longer leave
my projects unfinished'.

· <u>Make it in the here and now</u>
Write your affirmation in the
present tense: 'I finish my projects'
rather than 'I will finish my
projects'.

· <u>Describe the feeling</u>
Include some positive descriptors,
so that you can easily visualize
how great it feels to realize your
affirmation: 'I finish my projects
and I feel so satisfied.'

· <u>Evaluate</u> Does the affirmation you
wrote give you a positive feeling?
If so, wonderful! You have your
affirmation. If not, refine it. You may
need a 'stepping stone' to make your
affirmation more believable. For
example, if you have a complicated
track record with finishing what you
begin, your subconscious mind may
need more help believing 'I finish
my projects and I feel so satisfied'.
In that case try, 'I believe in the
possibility that I finish my projects
and feel satisfied', or 'I'm learning to
finish my projects with satisfaction
and ease'. With time and practice
you'll find that you no longer need
the stepping stone and you can
update your affirmation to 'I easily
finish my projects and I'm filled
with satisfaction!'

WAYS TO WORK WITH CRYSTALS

Crystals are a powerful force as they are but, in order to optimize their benefits, discover how to care for and recharge them with regular cleansing, and learn how to activate them using the intentions you've developed.

CLEANSE YOUR
CRYSTALS

Everything on Earth must go through a
process of decay and renewal. Cleansing your
crystals can help them reset with a clear energetic
frequency. When you cleanse a crystal, imagine
that you are clearing it of any energy that it may
have picked up from yourself, other people
and the environment.

How to Cleanse
Your Crystals

Make sure to research your stone to discover if the method you are considering is safe for both you and the crystal. For example, some crystals may dissolve in water or fade in sunlight. Some stones contain trace minerals that may be physically harmful when released into water.

Light: Place your crystal in sunlight or moonlight for an hour.
Salt: Immerse your crystal in salt for about five minutes.
Sound: Chant or use an instrument such as singing bowls, chimes or tuning forks.
Water: Wash your crystal under running water, from a natural water source or a tap, for a few minutes.
Visualization: Imagine crystalline light or archangels surrounding your crystal with the intention of cleansing.
Selenite: Place selenite next to your crystal and leave in place overnight.
Earth: Bury your crystal underground for about a day.

When to cleanse your crystals

It's a good idea to cleanse your crystal when you first get it and about once a month after that. Cleanse more often if you use your crystals regularly.

GROUND
YOURSELF

Before you do any kind of energy work, it's important to get grounded. When a ship puts down its anchor in a quiet harbour, it's protected from being pulled by strong waves back into the sea. As you engage in energy work with crystals, you may drift and dream far afield. It protects you to have an anchor that keeps you connected to the Earth.

How to Get
Grounded

· To begin, set yourself up in a quiet and comfortable space, either seated or lying down. Close your eyes. Imagine that your torso is like a tree trunk with roots growing down through your feet.

· Breathe comfortably and deeply as you imagine your roots flowing down through the ground and all the way to the Earth's core.

· Visualize a healing light moving up through your roots into your body. Imagine this healing light circulating through your body and carrying any tension or stress away and out, and back down into the Earth.

· Continue to imagine the energy flow – grounding energy coming up through your roots, tension and stress flowing back down to the Earth.

· When you feel relaxed and grounded, give thanks to the Earth before you open your eyes.

ACTIVATE YOUR
CRYSTALS

Now that your crystal is cleansed and you are grounded, you can 'program' your crystal with the intention you've developed. Programming your crystal is one way to activate it so that its vibrations are attuned to your desires and goals. It's as simple as telling your crystal what you intend to create or achieve.

How to Program
Your Intention

To amplify your crystal's power, focus your thoughts on your intention and train that energy towards your crystal.

- Make sure you have a clear intention or affirmation.

- Set a timer for ten minutes.

- Sit comfortably either in a chair or on the floor.

- Hold your crystal or place it on your body. You could also place it on the floor or on a table in front of you.

- On each inhale, repeat your intention out loud or in your mind.

- On each exhale bring your attention to your crystal.

- When you notice your attention wandering, bring your awareness back to the crystal and your breath.

- Repeat until your timer sounds.

VIRGO

DATES: AUGUST 23–SEPTEMBER 22 ELEMENT: EARTH
MODALITY: MUTABLE PLANET: MERCURY SYMBOL: VIRGIN
CRYSTAL: SAPPHIRE

YOUR SIGN,
EXPLAINED

Sensible, devoted, subtle Virgo. An alchemist at heart, you attend to each tiny detail until the final product is transcendent. Virgo is known as the Goddess of the Harvest – farmers place their crop at her feet and she devotedly sifts through each tiny bean and grain. When your labour is finished, the harvest gleams with perfection. Virgo's motto is 'I improve'. With immense wisdom you refine and improve the world, by finessing the tiny details. You're organized, grounded and present. It's easy for you to roll up your sleeves and devotedly set to work making the world a better place. Keeping everything flowing harmoniously helps you flourish. Through your efforts, you gain confidence in your abilities.

You have the ability to come back to the task at hand with enthusiasm and precision. This natural sense of devotion is inspiring. Elegant and classy, you have a subtle, natural gracefulness. For you, the beauty is in the details. This care for the details shows up in your excellent sense of style, and it also defines the way you like to work and play. You especially love activities that are finite, practical and actionable. You understand that daily habits and routines are what makes up a life. Your knack for paying attention and being present to the moment helps you feel satisfied with your lifelong journey.

With zippy Mercury as your ruling planet, your intellect is quick. You efficiently connect all the dots. Others appreciate that you communicate clearly and simply. You are an excellent teacher, meting out your profound wisdom in simple and palatable bites.

VIRGO IS
AN EARTH SIGN

Earth is the physical, the practical, the sensible and sensual. It's the ground beneath your feet. Logical and analytical, you sift through the world around you, making things better in a practical way. Like nature itself, you are constantly evolving.

VIRGO IS RULED BY
THE PLANET MERCURY

The fastest planet symbolizes the quick mental and electrical connections made in the brain and body. Mercury is the student, the scientist, the journalist and the intellectual. This is the part of you that analyzes and finds the best new solutions. You digest ideas, bringing thoughts into reality.

VIRGO IS AN
INTERPERSONAL SIGN

As the second of the three Earth signs, Virgo is an Interpersonal sign. Interpersonal signs lean out towards other people to experience the joy of connection. You yearn to be of service to others. When you can do something practical and real that helps someone else, the ground feels steady beneath your feet.

THE VIRGIN IS THE
SYMBOL FOR VIRGO

'Virgo' in Latin means maiden, young woman or virgin. Virgo in a modern interpretation is self-contained and self-sufficient, meaning that you are composed, poised and independent.

VIRGO IS A
MUTABLE SIGN

The Mutable signs adapt and shift. This energy keeps you ready to pivot, as you constantly refine and improve your productivity.

SAPPHIRE IS A KEY CRYSTAL
BIRTHSTONE FOR VIRGO

Sapphire is a calming crystal ally for all Virgos. This gleaming blue crystal helps you tune into the ocean of tranquillity that resides within you. Sapphire also strengthens the mind, helping you to gain insight and boost your self-discipline. Choose it as your go-to support when you need to de-stress or focus on something important.

VIRGO
TRAITS

Your key traits show how you shine.
These are the special characteristics
that make you unique.

Subtle   You're sweetly subtle, with an understated and tasteful manner. Your delicate style is on-point and refreshing.

Altruistic   Such a big heart! You love to give back to the world and to be of service.

Logical   With a razor-sharp mind, you display excellent critical thinking skills. You use these skills to problem-solve and draw useful conclusions.

Reliable   You are someone to count on. Responsible, dedicated and trustworthy, you take pride in your ability to follow through on your commitments.

Efficient   Running circles around everyone else, you are efficient and organized. You feel at your best when you're attending to every detail of daily life.

Perceptive   With your talent for critical thinking, you know how to focus on the heart of the matter.

Sensitive   You lead with your five senses. You are nature loving, appreciative of beauty, and very sensitive to the sights, sounds, smells, tastes and textures of your environment.

Classy   Naturally refined, you appreciate and radiate elegance.

VIRGO GIFTS
AND GROWTH AREAS

Your natural gifts offer both strengths and
challenges. The same traits that make you
special may also require balance at times.

Productive vs Perfectionist
A whirlwind of activity, you are
everywhere at once, getting everything
done. You have high standards for
yourself and others. Be wary of
unattainable perfectionism, which will
only serve to stress you out.

Reserved vs Repressed   You have a
soft-spoken approach. When you hold
back too much, your naturally reserved
nature can come across as repressed.

Giving vs Over-generous   You live to
give! You are truly kind, and being of
service to the world lights you up. Be
careful not to give too much, or you'll
start to feel burnt out.

Discerning vs Disapproving
For you, the beauty is in the details. You
have a discerning eye, and you use it to
improve the world around you. When
your passion for refining and improving
morphs into criticism, it's time to take a
break and focus on the big picture.

Analytical vs Anxious   Logical and
systematic, your intellect is on point.
When you use your analytical gifts to
try to sort through future unknowns,
anxiety and worry can flare. Try to focus
on the present moment.

Contained vs Compulsive   You strive
to fit all the elements of your life into
a proper order – for example, making
sure that your health and nutrition is
under control. When this tendency to
impose structure goes overboard, you
might find yourself falling into a pattern
of obsession or compulsion.

VIRGO
COMPATIBILITY

Compatibility is a complex feature of astrology because you are more than just your Sun sign. And other people are multi-faceted too.

Friends

With steady **Taurus** by your side, you can get almost anything done. You deftly wrangle with the myriad of details, while **Taurus** helps you remember what's most important.

Cancer meets you halfway in your goals of creating a productive and loving world. Your time spent together is a satisfying parade of to-do lists and errands.

When you want to go deep, follow a **Scorpio**. This water sign will ferry you into the passion, magic and mystery of life.

Let **Capricorn** keep track of the overall plan while you execute the tiny details. Together you make a brilliant team.

Foes

Virgo has a strong sense of duty and service, while **Aries** is speedy and impetuous. While you're still working and doing all the heavy lifting, **Aries** has already moved on.

Leo is flashy and over the top, while you're more refined. For this pairing to work, you either need to let loose a little bit more, or the Lion needs to tone it down.

With nothing solid to back up **Libra's** breezy words and compliments, you may find yourself doubting their sincerity.

Aquarius has an edgy and erratic side that ruffles your carefully arranged feathers. You love to put things in order, and **Aquarius** appreciates a bit of chaos.

| TAURUS | SCORPIO | ARIES | LIBRA |
| CANCER | CAPRICORN | LEO | AQUARIUS |

VIRGO
SUN

If you were born August 23–September 22, Virgo is your Sun sign (check your birth chart for an exact calculation). Your Sun sign describes your basic energy.

Just as the Sun is the centre of the solar system, your Sun sign (also called your zodiac sign or star sign) symbolizes the core of your being. As a Virgo Sun, you deeply value caring, competency and improvement. Integrity is important to you and integrity lives in the details. You know that for the project, relationship or event to work, you can't skip a step.

You sincerely care, and when you funnel your energy into practical actions that help other people, you experience true serenity. At times, you may need a reminder to get out of your head and listen to your heart.

Because your Sun sign fuels your confidence and enlivens your sense of self, there are two recommended crystals for Virgo Sun. The Amplifying crystal will help you expand upon your gifts and the Balancing crystal will help you integrate your growth areas.

VIRGO SUN
AMPLIFYING CRYSTAL

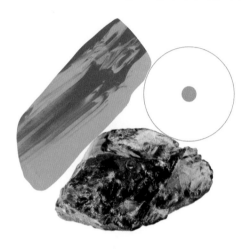

INTEGRITY,
SERENITY, FOCUS

Sapphire   Lean on Sapphire for its serene and calming energy. Spending time with this radiant blue crystal is like taking a dip in a still, clear pond. Everything slows down and you can immerse yourself in the moment. You have a natural ability to focus on the details, and sometimes that ability helps you get into 'the zone' – a rewarding and meditative state of mind. Sapphire may help you cultivate this mindset. And when you have more focus, your sense of determination increases as well. Keep Sapphire by your side when you want to practice a skill or craft, write a novel or organize your sock drawer.

Your 'true self' is the most authentic part of you. If you aren't always in touch with your true self, Sapphire can help make the introductions. And when you feel open to have an honest conversation with your real self, artifice and pretence slip away. You know exactly what matters to you and you can take small, persistent actions to help you act with integrity and feel aligned.

VIRGO SUN
BALANCING CRYSTAL

SELF-ACCEPTANCE,
LOVE, CONNECTION

Prasiolite   When you wish to turn down the volume on worry and self-criticism, look to Prasiolite. This green Amethyst helps you switch off the running commentary of your mind so that you can listen to your heart instead. With your heart leading the way, it becomes easy to feel compassion for yourself and others.

Reach for Prasiolite when you need to soothe anxiety, when you're feeling lonely, or when you're being hard on yourself. This loving stone rings the bell of acceptance and connection.

Prasiolite is a stone that helps you feel connected to nature, and this soothes your earthy Virgo spirit. If you crave the tranquillity of the natural world, but are living in an urban environment, Prasiolite can help you feel grounded and tuned into the earth.

VIRGO MOON

GOAL-SETTING, PEACEFULNESS, RESTORATION

In the same way that the Moon always appears to be changing shape in the sky, the Moon in your chart symbolizes the part of you that is always changing – your emotions.

Imagine that when you have an emotion come up, the Virgo part of you steps to centre stage. This happens throughout the day. It doesn't matter if the emotion is happiness, sadness, frustration or exhilaration – when emotions arise you go into full Virgo mode. Your methodical, careful, discerning, helpful side is activated. You focus on the details and you love to keep busy, using your hands and your brain to do something productive.

In emotional moments, you may find that you feel nervous or that your thoughts become self-critical. To counteract these tendencies you can use your gifts for being deliberate, logical and cautious. These strategies help you thrive.

You often turn inwards when you're emotional – your sign is self-contained and self-sufficient. Your analytical and discerning nature contributes to your helpful and healing demeanour. When a colleague, client, patient, friend or family member is in need of support or a clear perspective, you are ready to assist.

Nature soothes you, as does keeping your hands busy with cleaning or crafts. You're most supported by a crystal that helps you feel grounded while giving you a bit of perspective.

Moss Agate Moss Agate is a soft, sweet stone that opens the door to your dreams and goals and gently ushers you through. Lean on this crystal to feel balanced, centred and grounded when you are pushing or flailing in a situation. Moss Agate may help you zoom out and remember your bigger goals when you find yourself feeling overwhelmed by the details.

This glowing blue-green crystal echoes the peaceful pulse of nature and is perfectly attuned to your earthy sign. Feel refreshed and soothe your emotions with the help of Moss Agate.

VIRGO RISING

CLARITY, COMMUNICATION, FOCUS

Your Rising Sign is the sign that was on the eastern horizon when you were born. It represents the face you show to the world – your social personality. As a Virgo Rising, you flourish when you have the opportunity to be accurate and efficient. Your sense of vitality increases when you have a system of organization that allows you to imagine the possibilities and take clearly defined actions in pursuit of your goals.

Other people perceive you to be hard-working, caring, and practical. You are very 'hire-able' – everyone wants you on their team. When it comes to group endeavours, you are often found working hard in the background, although you have been known to take a leadership role when you feel very certain of your capabilities.

You are an excellent communicator, if a bit reserved. You light up when you feel sure of what you want to say, and you are building up the confidence required to share your perspective and put yourself out there.

Precision feels like heaven. When you have a handle on all of the details,

you truly thrive. You are learning to surf the waves of life with strength and finesse. Your best Virgo Rising crystal can help you amplify your naturally hard-working nature and find balance with an enhanced sense of ease and flow.

Blue Topaz Blue Topaz is a stone of the mind, which makes it perfect for your clever Virgo Rising. This sky-blue crystal boosts your ability to discern and communicate. The expressive potential this crystal offers is key, as it builds up your confidence so that you can share your ideas with others. Envision yourself standing proud, communicating what is most important to you. With Blue Topaz by your side, you enjoy a clear mind and a determined focus.

While this translucent crystal turns up mental clarity, it also calms and soothes the mind. When you need to cultivate a meditative state, or when you crave relaxation, turn to Blue Topaz.

OTHER VIRGO SUPPORT CRYSTALS

The following crystals are helpful for all Virgo placements – your Sun, Moon, Rising Sign and any other Virgo planet or point you may have in your chart. Harness the potential of these stones for clarity and ease in important life areas.

Everyone has different goals for romantic love. And your wishes or desires can change over time. You may wish to attract or pursue love. Perhaps you are hoping to deepen your ability to love, or open up to intimacy physically, emotionally or spiritually. Virgo, you have a huge heart and so much love to give. 'Give' is the key word here, as you show your love by doing helpful and caring things for others. When someone catches your heart, you work constantly on the relationship and for the relationship. You respond well to a lover who takes care not to overwhelm you and who acts with both passion and loyalty. You need a crystal that can bestow a dose of confidence in love, and that can stabilize you, so that you feel grounded in your relationships.

STABILITY
STRENGTH
PROTECTION

Almandine Garnet   The earthy, grounding energy offered by Almandine Garnet helps you feel stabilized. And with the nourishment of a stable 'root system', the more confidence you exude in your loving relationships. This newfound steadiness helps you attract new love or super-charge existing partnerships. Lean on this brownish-red crystal when you need to feel grounded and protected, begin a new partnership, or feel supported in a relationship.

VIRGO × FRIENDSHIP

With Virgo prominently placed in your chart, your reserved and serious nature makes you slow to take on new friendships. But when you do, you are loyal and attentive. You bring your friends the gifts of practicality, support, intellect and an understated but hilarious sense of humour. Although you expect your friends to live up to your high standards, you reciprocate in kind. You are an extraordinary listener. 'Supportive' is your middle name. Your friendship crystal can either help you be steady or go with the flow, even in overwhelming circumstances.

Pink Opal When it comes to friendship, you are already the full package. You only need support in soothing your heart. Your friendship crystal, Pink Opal, helps calm your anxiety and stops you feeling overwhelmed. With your emotions steadied, you are free to be yourself in your friendships. People tend to throw a lot at you, and your environment keeps you busy with lots to do and improve on. Let Pink Opal help you digest news and deal with other people's needs at your own pace, by buffering unnecessary urgency and replacing it with tranquillity.

SOOTHING

PEACE

BALANCE

Astrological insight can help galvanize your money-making potential. Your Virgo prosperity gifts are service, devotion, adaptability, precision, logic and kindness. If you'd like to make more money, look to these qualities for inspiration. What financial system helps you feel organized? How might you make your aptitude for helping others pay off financially? Can your penchant for data and details support your finances? As a Virgo, you may find that you have the energy to be very detailed in your money-management process. Reach out to a trusted advisor to help you with your big-picture goals or planning, and then follow through on the specifics.

OPEN-MINDEDNESS
ABUNDANCE
PROSPERITY

Sand Dollar Fossil Although not a crystal, Sand Dollar Fossil radiates with the energy of the Earth. These golden, coin-shaped relics bestow a feeling of prosperity and wealth. Let this fossil help you expand into a wide-open ocean of trust and possibility. And when your mind is open, you can discover new financial opportunities. As a Virgo, once you sense the possibilities, you need no help in working hard to attain them. You adapt and pivot with ease. Keep Sand Dollar Fossil nearby to remind you of this. Just like living sand dollars – who have evolved to be too tough for most predators to bother with – your natural ability to change and improve is constantly making you stronger.

VIRGO × WORK

Through your work, you create transcendent results. Like a baker measuring and perfecting, you bring together everyday ingredients to create an extraordinary confection. Everything flows when you define the actionable tasks, prepare your tools, and make your environment free from distractions. Then you can do what you do best – practice your craft, make the details shine, analyze, compile, edit and sort. Your work energy comes from your love of the small tasks that add up to a transformational outcome. The last ingredient you need is drive – fire yourself up with warmth and enthusiasm with the help of your Virgo work crystal.

Peridot Peridot is gem-quality Olivine and is a crystal of joyful action. Instead of getting stuck in rumination, let this yellow-green stone propel you forwards with enthusiasm. Who are you and where are you going? Get your answers to these questions through playfully doing what you love. The warmth of this sunny crystal helps you feel hopeful about your big-picture goals, so that you can confidently focus on the daily tasks. Feel certain of your life path and skip joyfully through the steps of your work day with the support of Peridot.

**WARMTH
CERTAINTY
WELL-BEING**

As a Virgo, health and well-being are very important to you. In fact, your sign rules the medical profession. When it comes to your health, you tend to be proactive. Because you are always calculating the effects of your choices, your overall health benefits. This hyper-awareness is usually a good thing, but can become a challenge when research and planning skews towards worrying or overthinking. If you worry too much about potential health outcomes, you might even find yourself with hypochondriac tendencies. Instead, put as much energy into calming your nervous system as you put into taking care of your body and you will feel grounded, balanced and serene. A soothing and relaxing crystal can help you recharge.

SOOTHING
MEDITATIVE
PROTECTION

Amethyst Amethyst resonates with soothing peace and harmony. When you need to step away from a busy day, turn to Amethyst and meditate for a moment. This dreamy crystal can help you drift away from the mundane moments of life and connect with your hopes and intuition. If your mind is racing, or you're feeling overwhelmed, reach for Amethyst. This radiant purple stone protects and calms the spirit, resulting in general health and well-being.

VIRGO
THROUGHOUT
THE YEAR

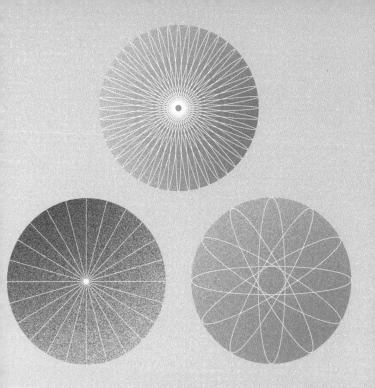

The energies of the zodiac signs affect us throughout the year. In astrology, there is a season for everything. Feeling separated from nature's cycles and rhythms can make you feel out of step or off-kilter. It may add to stress and drain energy. Understanding and attuning to astrology's seasons might help you feel enlivened.

Take this attunement one step further by using crystals to amplify the unique energy of each moment, so that you feel fully aligned with the rhythms of nature.

The following pages take you on a journey with the sun as it passes through the twelve signs of the zodiac on its annual rotation. You will discover the key energies of each season, along with a sign-specific horoscope that aligns with the important themes of your unique chart.

CONFIDENCE AND LEADERSHIP

Aries season is the signal that begins the horse race. And they're off! This is the moment to gallop at top speed towards your goals. Put yourself out there with confidence. Make bold decisions and step in time with your intuition. This season is about saying YES to who you are and living your life with freedom. The buds are beginning to emerge and new life is beginning. Sync up with this feeling of potential and possibility.

VIRGO HOROSCOPE FOR ARIES SEASON

The Sun is lighting up your area of trust, intimacy and transformation. These are tricky and touchy topics. When you build up your confidence you feel empowered to trust others.

When you trust others, you have opportunities to create intimacy and union. Through exploring these themes, you may encounter transformation and growth.

Affirmation	
I AM ENOUGH AND I AM READY.	

Morning Practice	**Evening Practice**
Get your heart rate up with some fiery cardio exercise.	Cool down that inner fire with a soothing herbal tea.

CRYSTALS FOR
ARIES SEASON

CONFIDENCE

Hessonite Garnet   Developing confidence is a practice of establishing deep self-trust. Let Hessonite Garnet's activating and powerful energy help you build up your courage so that you can just go for it. Also try Green Aventurine, Orange Calcite or Malachite.

LIVING BOLDLY

Pink Aventurine   When the time is ripe for taking bold action, Pink Aventurine can help you advance into your next adventure. Reach for it when you need a boost of fun. This spirited crystal connects you with your heart centre, and acts as your best accomplice in bravery and boldness. Or choose Ruby, Tangerine Quartz or Sardonyx.

DRIVE

Fire Agate   Aries season is the vehicle in which to follow your passions and desires, which makes Fire Agate the gasoline. Whether you need to get an important project going or just tackle spring cleaning, put yourself on track to get things done by syncing up with the vibration of this fierce crystal. You could also reach for Bloodstone, Stromatolite or Cinabrite.

MONEY AND
SELF-WORTH

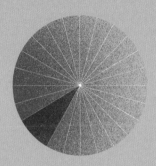

Like working in a garden and then enjoying the beauty that you've cultivated, Taurus represents sustained effort that leads to a productive reward. This season is the prime time to focus on building up your sense of personal worth and value. On one level, this process may involve nurturing your self-esteem. On another level, this may include thinking about security, money and finances. Taurus season is also a time to remember the beauty of life. It reminds us that no matter what is going on, there are simple pleasures to be had.

VIRGO HOROSCOPE
FOR TAURUS SEASON

It's time to broaden your perspective and expand your mind. The Sun is touring your zone of expansion, hope and enthusiasm. Positive thinking could be something you choose to focus on right now. With a strong sense of optimism, you may find that you feel fired up to take action. During this joyful time, explore your key values and remember what inspires you.

Morning Practice	**Evening Practice**
Practice gratitude by reminding yourself of three things you're grateful for.	Do something that feels good to your body, like stretching or wearing soft clothing.

CRYSTALS FOR TAURUS SEASON

MONEY MAGIC

Green Jade   No matter where you are beginning financially, Green Jade will juice up your money situation. This abundance stone has a way of amplifying your potential. A soft and expansive prosperity stone that soothes the spirit, it will support you as you make wise financial decisions. Reach for it when you crave a feeling of security. You could also use Pyrite, Emerald or Epidote.

SELF-WORTH

Red Jasper   Red Jasper will amp up your self-appreciation quotient. Choose Red Jasper when you're feeling uncertain, if your confidence could use a boost, or if you want to feel more resilient in any way. This stone will get you in the groove of trusting your own value. Also try Carnelian, Chrysocolla or Bixbite.

ABUNDANCE

Green Apatite   If you are feeling like something in your life is lacking, such as money, time, energy, sleep, or support, for example, you might need to boost your sense of abundance. Taurus season is the perfect time to grasp hold of that feeling of nature's plentifulness. Use Green Apatite to replenish your energy and help you feel satisfied and satiated with what you have. You could also reach for Golden Tourmaline, Uvarovite Garnet or Agate.

VALUES
AND COMMUNITY

Gemini energy is like a buzzing bee that moves from flower to flower in a garden. This season is a time of mental stimulation, new ideas, learning, communicating and sharing. Use Gemini season to evaluate or challenge your mindset and values. Which attitudes are no longer serving you? What's truly important to you? Gemini season is also a time to connect with others in the community. What can you learn from others? What can you teach others? It's a fun and lively season full of new connections.

VIRGO HOROSCOPE
FOR GEMINI SEASON

Focus on your goals and ambitions. Your career, or perhaps your public image, demands your attention. Determine what you want to achieve and follow through on a detailed plan to make it happen. You can use the current energy to help you systematize and strategize. There is work to be done and you are the right person to make it happen.

Morning Practice	**Evening Practice**
Help a new mindset emerge with a potent Gemini season intention.	Before falling asleep, envision yourself having a great time at a party surrounded by everyone you love.

CRYSTALS FOR GEMINI SEASON

MASTER YOUR MINDSET

Heliodor   Have repeating thoughts, fears or anxieties been plaguing you? Use the revitalizing energy of Gemini season and Heliodor to hit the reset button on these old thought patterns. This stone will gently help you harmonize your thoughts and adjust your mindset, helping you reconnect with your true values. Alternatively, try Blue Lace Agate, Chrome Chalcedony or Dragonstone.

CONNECTING

Agatized Coral   When you really want to feel connected, seen, heard and understood, reach for Agatized Coral. This fossilized coral nudges you to reach out to others and helps you analyse your relationships, whether with friends, lovers, family, neighbours or colleagues. It relays an upbeat feeling so that you can view your relationships with the people in your life with optimism. You may also choose Citrine, Apricot Agate or Bismuth.

COMMUNICATION

Aquamarine   Aquamarine is your crystal-clear communication companion. Communication helps us feel connected, and allows us to learn and grow. In those moments when you feel confused or foggy, this elegant stone will help you become grounded and steady. Use Aquamarine to find your voice – it will help you tune into your own true message and the truth of those around you. Alternatively, reach for Turquoise, Prairie Tanzanite or Green Chrysocolla.

55

HOME AND NURTURE

Come on home to Cancer season. Like Cancer's symbol, the Crab, wrap yourself in a protective shell and reflect on your life and your feelings. In Cancer season, engage in meaningful self-care, and also put your energy into nurturing others. Discover what makes you feel safe and cosy. This could be your actual home, your closest relationships or tending to the feelings and needs of your inner child.

VIRGO HOROSCOPE FOR CANCER SEASON

The moment is ripe for dreaming up an exciting future. Transfer your dreams from your heart to your mind by creating a clear mental picture of what it is you wish for. The Sun is moving through your zone of hopes and aspirations for the future. Write, draw, collage or brainstorm to create a clear image of your dreams.

Morning Practice	Evening Practice
Let your inner child take the lead: what do they want to do today?	Sing a lullaby to soothe your inner child before bed.

CRYSTALS FOR CANCER SEASON

NURTURING

Blue Calcite   What do you want to actively care for? Yourself? A child? A creative project? In order to feel truly nurturing, you need to feel inspired by love. Blue Calcite will help you soften and open up your heart centre, so that you feel drawn to put your compassionate and attentive energy where it is needed most. Other nurturing crystals include Moonstone, Blue Chalcedony and Bumblebee Jasper.

HOME ENVIRONMENT

Pink Mangano Calcite   Home is where you are safe and protected. It's your emotional nest where you can relax. Use Pink Mangano Calcite to create a grounded and peaceful home environment. This stone acts as a balm that will help you feel harmonized. Place this rosy crystal in your inner sanctum and set the intention to soothe conflict and soften your environment so that you can restore your energy after a long day or week. You could also try Chiastolite, Rose Quartz or Peach Moonstone.

FAMILY BONDS

Bornite   Family, whether chosen or blood-related, represent some of our closest relationships. Use Bornite to foster the strength of family relationships. This is a joyful stone that will help you embrace the positives that come from your family circle, while at the same time grounding you to help you remember who you are as an individual. Also try Orange Calcite, Indigo Gabbro or Girasol Quartz.

CREATIVITY
AND FUN

Harnessing your creativity and expressing your
true self with others, that's the key to making the most of Leo
season. It's all about playful sharing and creative shining.
Radiate your magnificent heart of gold outwards with
immediacy, freedom, spontaneity, generosity and a giant
sense of fun. During this season of wholehearted
self-expression, take a little time to remember how unique
you are. Remember what inspires you and reflect on what
you love most about yourself.

VIRGO HOROSCOPE
FOR LEO SEASON

There is a challenge available to you, should you choose to accept it. And that is to unplug, retreat and let go. Just for now, give up on your to-do list and your responsibilities. The Sun is nudging you to connect with your inner world. Let yourself float and drift in the realm of feelings, imagination and dreams. Find peace within.

Affirmation

MY CREATIVE SELF IS
COMING OUT TO PLAY.

Morning Practice

Create daily.

Evening Practice

Seek out a chance to laugh every day and go to bed with a smile on your face.

INSPIRATION

Rutilated Quartz   Inspiration is the creative spark and Rutilated Quartz can help you turn that spark into a roaring bonfire. Make Leo season feel lit up with creativity. Keep Rutilated Quartz by your side when you need an inventive solution to a problem at work, when your love life could use an inspiring reboot, or when you are ready to awaken the artist within. Set your intentions and let this highly programmable stone carry the flame of your dreams. You could also use Sunstone, Golden Labradorite or Yellow Sapphire.

SELF-APPRECIATION

Thulite   Leo season is the time to shed all insecurities and put your faith in your one true self. Loving yourself dissolves insecurity and self-criticism. Thulite tunes you into the vibration of love, peace and harmony, allowing you to be present and wholly yourself. Alternatively, reach for Ruby, Larimar, or Desert Jasper.

COURAGE

Golden Apatite   To ensure your lion-heartedness knows no bounds, you need to fire up your courage. Golden Apatite bestows upon you both passion and discernment, which determine which fears are baseless. Use it when you need to take a risk at work, strike up a conversation with someone you admire or stand up for your values. Other courage-giving crystals are Carnelian, Iolite-Sunstone or Citrine.

HEALTH
AND HABITS

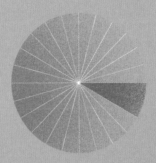

Our goals and dreams require a big-picture view,
but Virgo season reminds us that life is actually lived in the
small details. Focus on how you are living your life, your
everyday routines and rituals. On a practical level, what is
important to you? Virgo energy helps you take a closer
look at your health and habits, and how you can be
of service to others as well.

VIRGO HOROSCOPE
FOR VIRGO SEASON

Let the real you shine. The Sun is
traversing your zone of identity and
personality. Take this opportunity
to get reacquainted with the special
ingredients that make up your persona.

Spend a little time discovering how
you'd like to shine out into the world.
Express yourself with boldness
and delight.

Morning Practice	**Evening Practice**
Drink a glass of water first thing.	Write down one task you're going to complete tomorrow, and stick to it.

CRYSTALS FOR VIRGO SEASON

FOCUS

Clear Quartz   Virgo season ushers in a chance to notice the details and get focused. Use Clear Quartz to take you all the way there. This cleansing stone helps you rivet your attention on your commitments. When you program Clear Quartz with your intention for focus, you'll find that it supports you, whether you have a tight deadline or you just really need to concentrate. You could also turn to Vanadinite, Amazonite or Tiger Iron.

HEALTH

Chevron Amethyst   A lot of factors go into maintaining optimum health: genetics, diet, exercise, access to care, to name just a few. Virgo season energy will encourage you to think wisely about the preventative measures that you can take to boost both your mental well-being and physical health. Use Chevron Amethyst for gentle motivation that can help you happily embrace healthier choices. Or try Girasol Quartz, Ruby Fuchsite or Black Tourmaline.

ALTRUISM

Stromatolite   Humanity wouldn't be a successful species without the desire to be of service to others. Virgo season plus Stromatolite is your recommendation for kindness and selfless action. Turn your attention to what you can do to help others, whether that's volunteering, making a donation to a good cause, or simply smiling and being friendly. Let Stromatolite amplify your altruistic nature. Alternatively, reach for Stichtite, Rhodonite or Rose Quartz.

RELATIONSHIPS
AND BALANCE

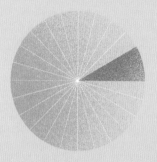

Libra season is symbolized by balanced scales.
It's a chance to look at all life areas and judge the
equilibrium. Are your relationships in balance? Do both
people in your relationships have what they want and
need? This can be a fun and harmonious time to socialize.
During Libra season, balance can also be created in your
environment through art, decoration and organization.
The scales are the symbol for justice and Libra season brings
a collective yearning to make the systems of government
more fair and to expose inequalities.

VIRGO HOROSCOPE
FOR LIBRA SEASON

It's time to turn your attention to
money and worth as the Sun is touring
your area of stability and resources. In
astrology, the area of worth (money)
is also the area of self-worth, and both
are linked with stability. Dig down into
your thoughts, beliefs and experiences
and discover what makes you feel
worthy and stable. Build upon these
themes throughout Libra season.

Morning Practice

Reach out and message
someone who is important to
you, and tell them why.

Evening Practice

Meditate to create
mental balance.

CRYSTALS FOR
LIBRA SEASON

HEALTHY BOUNDARIES

Iolite   Communicating what you want, need and desire is a
great starting point to gain clarity in your relationships. Iolite
can help you reflect and get to know yourself – the first step to
speaking and sharing your truth with others. Once your inner
base is stabilized, Iolite can help you reach out to another
person, while maintaining your own healthy boundaries. This
healing stone has a peaceful energy that helps you create
balance between yourself and a partner. You could also use
Amazonite, Purple Jade or Chiastolite.

BALANCE

Shungite   Balance is an active state, requiring constant
adjustment. It comes under the jurisdiction of the intellectual,
analytical sign of Libra. Keep checking in with yourself
throughout Libra season to determine what needs more
balance. For a crystal that will help you stay steady, reach for
Shungite. Or choose Diopside, Selenite or Turquoise.

DECISIVENESS

Ametrine   Libra season is an excellent time to analyse, think
things through and come up with new ideas. Keep Ametrine
by your desk for productive planning sessions and for when you
have big decisions to make. This balancing stone will help you
keep your life on track. As an alternative, try Variscite, Fluorite
or White Sapphire.

TRANSFORMATION AND FORGIVENESS

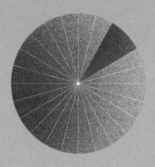

Scorpio season pulls you deeper – emotionally, physically and spiritually. This is a season of transformation, helping you to feel deeply, release old emotions and thought patterns, and get ready to move on to the next stage. By pulling back the layers and being honest with the truth of who you are, it's also an opportunity to deepen your relationships with others by letting them get to know the real you.

VIRGO HOROSCOPE FOR SCORPIO SEASON

The Sun is nudging you to connect with your inner world as it moves through your zone of mindset and community. Your mindset is like the soil that nurtures all of your thoughts and ideas. Make sure the soil is healthy by talking things through with trusted friends. Writing down your ideas may also help you gain clarity. As this is a time when your mind is open and activated, you may even seek out new ways of thinking.

Morning Practice	**Evening Practice**
Forgive yourself for something.	Forgive someone else for something.

CRYSTALS FOR SCORPIO SEASON

INTIMACY

Red Tourmaline Scorpio season propels you to create warmth and closeness. But opening yourself up to the vulnerability of intimacy demands courage. Whether you are setting the stage for sexual intimacy or emotional intimacy, Red Tourmaline will help you feel confident enough to embrace deep connection with others. Other crystals for intimacy are Garnet, Shiva Lingam or Red Aventurine.

TRANSFORMATION

Moldavite Transformation brings both endings and new beginnings. Moldavite will help you spiritually and emotionally adjust when change comes into your life – when a relationship has run its course, a shift is needed in the work arena or a new adventure calls your name. When the transformation you are undergoing is more subtle in texture, like saying goodbye to an old habit, Moldavite will help you align with your new reality. Or try Shungite, Moss Agate or Tugtupite.

FORGIVENESS

Dioptase Whether you need to be kinder to yourself or let go of hurt that someone else has caused you, forgiveness doesn't happen all at once. It's a process that you set in motion. Finding forgiveness requires self-love, self-worth and understanding. Dioptase can help you practice forgiveness by supporting you with its gentle and loving vibrations. You could also turn to Black Moonstone, Rhodochrosite or Pink Tourmaline.

WISDOM
AND FREEDOM

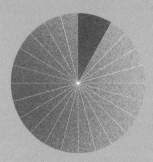

Sagittarius season is represented by the archer who shoots high and blazes a trail into new territory. The archer is also a centaur – half horse and half human, half wild and half philosophical. Sagittarius season is a time to feel fiercely alive and simultaneously inspired to ask big, existential questions. It's a season for expanding your boundaries and traveling physically and mentally to understand more about the world and the human experience.

VIRGO HOROSCOPE
FOR SAGITTARIUS SEASON

Float in the world of emotions and feelings. The Sun is moving through your area of home and family. Notice what makes you feel safe and supported. Get cosy and nurture yourself. Pay attention to the relationships you share with those in your inner circle. If these relationships are supportive, lean into them and receive the care and attention that warms your heart.

Morning Practice	**Evening Practice**
Go for a walk or a jog out in nature.	Memorize an inspiring quote.

CRYSTALS FOR SAGITTARIUS SEASON

INNER WISDOM

Azurite   In Sagittarius season, the archer knows that the best way to take aim is to trust your inner wisdom. When you are connected to your true self, it's easier to make choices. Life feels more satisfying. Azurite is the stone to hold and carry when you want to bolster your self-confidence and tune into your wisdom. Or choose Idocrase, Shattuckite or Amethyst.

EXPANSION

Jasper   Ruled by the gas giant Jupiter, Sagittarius is the sign of expansion. During this season, you can move beyond anything that is limiting you. Is there an area of your life in which you feel trapped in a cage? Maybe if you take a closer look, you'll find that the door to the cage has been open the entire time. Feel the freedom and expansion that is available to you with the help of Jasper. This enlivening stone will help you break out into new territory. Alternatives are Blue Topaz, Pink Chalcedony or Ruby Iolite.

ADVENTURE AND TRAVEL

Turquoise   When you're setting out in search of new horizons, reach for Turquoise as your talisman for protection and luck. Travel and adventure require equal parts bravery and boldness, but the reward is an expanded mindset and perspective. Let Turquoise be your steady support system as you push beyond your boundaries to discover excitement, new opportunity and enlightenment. You could also use Green Opal, Smoky Quartz or Aventurine.

CAREER
AND GOALS

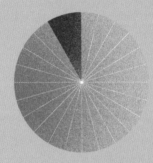

Like the mountain goat, in Capricorn season
you are primed to choose your footing carefully as
you make your ascent. Capricorn season brings practical
and productive forward motion. Use this energy efficiently
and tactically. You may choose to counterbalance this drive
and ambition with a large dose of acceptance, both
of yourself and others. Remember to give yourself a
break; you are trying your best.

VIRGO HOROSCOPE
FOR CAPRICORN SEASON

With the Sun moving through your sector of fun, play and creativity, it's time for you to enjoy yourself. Turn everything into a game. Remember what it's like to play and lose track of time. You might currently find yourself drawn to art, music, comedy, cooking, gardening or fashion – anything that allows you to feel creative and radiant.

Morning Practice

Write down your goals.

Evening Practice

Reflect on your
accomplishments.

CRYSTALS FOR
CAPRICORN SEASON

ACHIEVEMENT

Fluorite   Your Capricorn season recommendation supports
you in taking things one step at a time while staying focused
on your big picture goals. Look to Fluorite. Fluorite's unique
vibration can help you concentrate, while energizing you so
that you can keep moving forward. Or look for support from
Ocean Jasper, Septarian Nodule or Tiger's Eye.

CAREER

Cat's Eye   Capricorn season is a wonderful time to take
stock. While you think about your work life, keep Cat's Eye by
your side. This stone helps you know your strengths, which is
imperative for a fulfilling career. It will help you feel optimistic
and believe in yourself. Cat's Eye's structured energy helps
you know your personal boundaries and make smart money
choices. You could also use Andradite Garnet, Apatite or
Hawk's Eye.

FOR SELF-ACCEPTANCE

Blue Aragonite   Let calming Blue Aragonite guide you
when you need to feel the soothing balm of self-acceptance.
Capricorn season pushes you to achieve, which may cause
you to question your progress in life. Counterbalance that by
learning to accept yourself for who you are. Blue Aragonite
has a compassionate energy that may inspire you to be less
judgemental towards yourself and show yourself more kindness.
Other crystals for self-acceptance are Prasiolite, Amethyst
or Shungite.

FRIENDSHIP
AND VISION

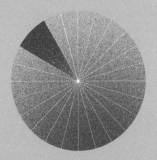

Aquarius season pushes people and ideas to the
forefront. What are your big ideas for the future?
And who is in your community? Your vision for the future
may also be a vision for humanity. Take the time to research
causes to which you might contribute time, money and
resources. Your friends, communities and social groups are
extra important during this season, so prioritize the people
who mean the most to you.

VIRGO HOROSCOPE
FOR AQUARIUS SEASON

The Sun is touring your sector of health
and organization. Virgo, this is a chance
for you to focus on your routines, habits
and systems – and make sure all are up
to your high standards. Deal with your
to-do list. Align your habits with your
goals. Get all systems operational and
you will feel filled with pristine joy.

Morning Practice

Create a vision board and make it the
first thing you see when you wake up.

Evening Practice

Call a friend for a
meaningful chat.

CRYSTALS FOR
AQUARIUS SEASON

FRIENDSHIP

Bismuth   Aquarius season asks you to turn towards your
community. What can you offer? What will you receive?
Friends enrich your life in so many ways, but mostly by
encouraging your feeling of belonging – a natural mood
booster. Bismuth has an expansive energy that helps you join
with others in a shared sense of community. Carry Bismuth as a
reminder that you are connected to others. Or you could reach
for Carnelian, Sunset Sodalite or Blue Apatite.

FAITH IN THE FUTURE

Cavansite   The future is uncertain. Sometimes you need a
boost to help you trust in the potential and possibility of what
the future can become. In that case, reach for Cavansite.
This stone has a sweet vibe of positivity that can give you the
courage to believe in your biggest dreams for the future. Some
alternatives are Peridot, Muscovite or Auralite 23.

VIBRATIONAL LIFT

Apophyllite   When Aquarius season asks you to turn
your attention to what is possible, it helps to have a positive
outlook. Without suppressing any challenging feelings (those
are important and need to be processed), pay some special
attention to the positive things in your life and work to create
an enduring, positive mindset. If you need a little extra support,
reach for Clear or Green Apophyllite. This high-vibe crystal
can lift your spirits and help you feel full of potential. You
could also try Quartz, Hematite or Angelite.

INTUITION AND SPIRITUALITY

The most mystical season of all, Pisces season is the time to tune into your intuition. Slide like a slippery fish into the sphere of your dreams, faith, spirituality, compassion and creativity. This is a moment to rest, reflect and look inwards. Reconnect with your imagination. Feel your feelings. Plug into your spirituality or whatever makes you feel connected to the universe.

VIRGO HOROSCOPE FOR PISCES SEASON

Your focus is placed on partnership – the delicate balance of 'me' and 'you'. Work on being a really good listener. When you honour another person's experience, you give them an incredible gift. You don't need to fix anything or offer advice, it's your steady presence and compassion that is needed. Make sure that you have opportunities to receive the same compassion from another person.

Morning Practice

Record your dreams.

Evening Practice

Do some freewriting
to clear your mind.

CRYSTALS FOR PISCES SEASON

COMPASSION

Lavender Quartz   Lavender Quartz helps you feel peace and
understanding for others. It will bestow upon you the softness
that you need to open up to other people's perspectives. It will
also allow you to dissolve drama with a heightened sense of
empathy. This soothing and healing stone can offer strength
while you stand in someone else's shoes. A compassionate life
is a fulfilling life. As an alternative, turn to Thulite, Prehnite
with Epidote or Fluorite.

INTUITION

Pink Opal   When you trust your inner guidance system you
have ultimate clarity. Harness the power of your intuition
in Pisces season with the help of Pink Opal. This stone will
help you connect to yourself and to your guides. It raises
the volume on your inner 'Yes' or 'No' by quietening any
distractions and helping you connect within. Other crystals
for intuition are Clear Quartz, Moldavite or Dumortierite.

FOR FAITH

Celestite   Faith can be thought of as a complete trust or
confidence in someone or something. With a little bit of
faith you may find it easier to contend with fear or anxiety.
But trust and faith must be developed from within. In Pisces
season, harness the power of high-vibrational Celestite to
help you move beyond unnecessary fears as you put your
trust in something bigger. You could also use Vatican Stone,
Apophyllite or Turquoise.

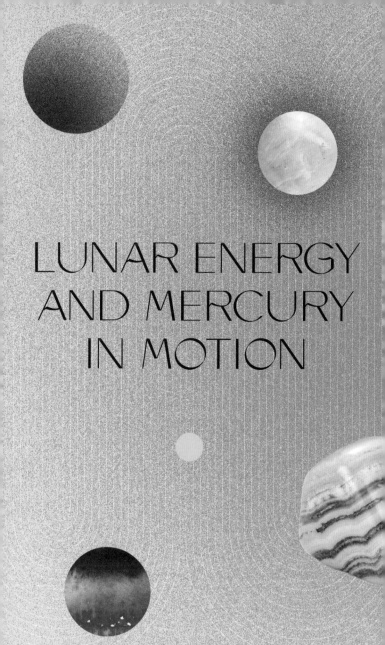

LUNAR ENERGY AND MERCURY IN MOTION

THE LUNAR
CYCLE

In astrology, the Moon is a catalyst, helping us to move
forwards with our goals and intentions.

The 29-day lunar cycle begins in darkness. The Moon
then appears as a faint crescent and grows bigger until it's
full. This process, from darkness to Full Moon, mirrors the
incubation and development of your own creative process.
Then, the Moon wanes until it completely disappears,
reflecting another stage of the creative cycle – the process of
releasing your efforts and making space for another cycle to
begin. This allows new thoughts and ideas to emerge.

Each of the eight phases of the Moon cycle offers a
different type of energy, which we will explore in this
chapter. You can follow the Moon through the lunar month
with crystal recommendations, setting your intentions in
alignment with the New Moon and letting the lunar cycle
help you make that intention into reality. The lunar cycle
will also help you cleanse and release so that you can gently
transition into the next phase.

By using crystals to work with the lunar cycle you can
activate the potential of the Moon and amplify its energy.
Through visualization or meditation, tap into the unique
energies of each stage of the Moon cycle with the following
crystals. For the suggested rituals at each phase, choose a
crystal from the recommended options, or substitute with
your favourite crystal.

Sun

New Moon

Waxing Crescent

Waning Crescent

First Quarter

Third Quarter

Earth

Waxing Gibbous

Waning Gibbous

Full Moon

NEW MOON

SET YOUR NEW INTENTIONS

The Moon is dark. This is a time for
reflection and a time to connect with
your inner self. Use your energy to
envision what you would like to make
happen. What do you desire? What
are your dreams? Anything is possible
– imagine that you are planting seeds
of intention that will manifest and
grow throughout the Waxing Moon
Phase. The New Moon is a quiet and
emotional time and you may discover
that, as you think about what you would
like to create, many different feelings
arise. Excitement, anticipation, fear,
worry – whatever feelings arise, make
space for those feelings and be gentle
with yourself. Listen to your intuition
and imagine your next steps.

Black Moonstone can support you
during the delicate and sensitive New
Moon vibration. It offers wellsprings of
patience and peace as you work with
your emotions and reflect on your life.
When your dreams are germinating
under the surface, Black Moonstone
can help you trust your own process.

Labradorite opens your third eye wide
so that you can tune into your intuition,
and design your goals in accordance
with your path and purpose.

Pink Sapphire's loving energy
can buffer you and help you feel
emotionally at ease.

Ametrine provides sweet joy and
concentrated focus so that you can set
intentions with confidence.

TRUST,
INSPIRATION, SERENITY
AND DELIGHT

New Moon Ritual

Freewrite about what you yearn for and anything else that's on
your mind. Then jot down your intentions for this Moon cycle
on a piece of paper and place your chosen crystal on top.

WAXING CRESCENT
NURTURE YOUR INTENTIONS

Your seeds of intention are germinating under the soil, and maybe some of the plants are just beginning to sprout. As the lunar energy builds momentum, make sure that you have the resources you need to achieve your goals. Provide structure and support for yourself. This cycle is just beginning to take shape, so consider how your choices will determine your direction – maybe there are changes you'd like to make to your goals. Remain curious throughout this process, because anything is possible!

TRUTH, INTUITION, MANIFESTATION AND FOCUS

Turquoise is a powerhouse of a crystal that can deftly carry you through the precarious Waxing Crescent phase. At this moment you need a subtle combination of confidence, discernment, curiosity and commitment. Turquoise can help you understand the truth of what you need to create, and it can help you stay open and accepting of your process. Use this stone as you decide what you really want to manifest and commit to during this Moon cycle.

Shattuckite helps you intuitively illuminate your path so that you can make the decisions that are right for you.

Pyrite offers crystalline protection and is a wonderful choice to help you realize your goals.

Orange Calcite gives you mental focus and lots of energy for the journey ahead.

Waxing Crescent Moon Ritual

Read and rewrite your intentions for this Moon cycle.
Decorate the paper and place your chosen crystal back on top.

BUILD YOUR MOMENTUM

Look around your garden of intentions and discover what is growing. Have your goals started to take shape? If so, how are they coming along? Do you need more support? Perhaps you have had surprising results? At the First Quarter Moon the constraints of reality can be intimidating. You have big dreams, but sometimes you encounter resistance when dreams make contact with real world limitations. Maybe there is more work required than you had foreseen, or there are real-world issues with time, money, support or other resources. Give yourself lots of encouragement. Pivot, and reassess if necessary. This is an exciting, high energy time, so keep taking action and building momentum.

Bumblebee Jasper When reality, and all of its limitations, hits, Bumblebee Jasper can help you stay the course with confidence. Lean on this crystal when you need the energy to just keep moving forward. It will subdue your fears and inspire you to push past your comfort zone.

Peridot is a cheery companion that will help you look at any situation with optimism.

Tangerine Quartz offers creative potential that makes problem solving effortless.

Aventurine will vitalize you and give you the confidence to keep going.

CONFIDENCE,
OPTIMISM, CREATIVITY AND
VITALITY

First Quarter Moon Ritual

Light a candle, hold your chosen crystal and
visualize your intentions being realized.

DEVELOP YOUR INTENTIONS

It's astonishing what a little effort can create! Now that you've made it to the Waxing Gibbous phase of the Moon cycle, you are starting to see the effects of the intentions that you set. If your goal was to improve your nutrition, you may be feeling better already. If you felt motivated to get out there and start dating, you may have started some new conversations. Whatever the last few days have revealed, now is the time to roll up your sleeves and actively give shape to your garden. What will you weed out? What is working, and what isn't working? What changes might you make? The intensity has almost peaked so take tender care of your emotional well-being as you keep putting in effort towards your dreams.

Jet Jet's grounding energy will help you establish deep root systems for your developing intentions. When you need strength and motivation to keep pushing forwards with your goals, this stone will support you. As a bonus, jet has a sheltering vibration that can steady you emotionally and help you surge forwards with optimism and hope.

Hematite offers balance and protection, helping you proactively take care of yourself during this active time.

Carnelian lights your fire with sparkling enthusiasm and convinces you to tune into your creative side.

Blue Lace Agate calms your mind, allowing you to weed through your options and make solid decisions.

GROUNDING,
PROTECTION, ENTHUSIASM
AND PEACE OF MIND

Waxing Gibbous Moon Ritual

While holding or wearing your chosen crystal, do something that feels active or expressive, such as dancing, painting, gardening, cooking or singing. Imagine your goals and repeat your intentions.

HARVEST

Everything is revealed under the light of the Moon. The attempts you've made, your wins, your losses. It's time to get out in the garden and harvest the crop. Regardless of whether the bounty lives up to your expectations, there is something to appreciate and celebrate. At the Full Moon, honour what you've created and give gratitude to yourself for your commitment. This phase represents the push and pull of two opposite energies as the Moon is in the opposite sign to the Sun. The result is a highly polarized and intense energy that can heighten emotions, pull you in two different directions, or cause you to realize something important. Make sure to be very gentle with yourself and those around you.

White Moonstone symbolizes the Full Moon and all of its glorious creativity and excitement. This pearly white crystal shines a bright light so that you can see clearly. As you examine the fruits that you've cultivated during the Waxing Moon phase, use the receptive and healing energy of White Moonstone to help you accept and celebrate. It's time for gratitude, and this comforting crystal will help you open up to that feeling.

Green Apatite is an antidote to the drama of the Full Moon – use it to highlight joy and abundance.

Jade has a subtle, soothing energy that imparts an optimistic attitude.

Stilbite connects the heart, mind and intuition – this can help you rationally balance your emotions while still opening up to divine insight.

EMOTIONAL EXPLORATION,
ABUNDANCE, PEACEFULNESS
AND RECEPTIVITY

Full Moon Ritual

Hold your chosen crystal and write down three things that you are grateful for. The Full Moon is also a great time to cleanse your crystals. Place them outside or on a windowsill and let them bathe in the Moon's healing energy.

REFLECT AND REVIEW

Now that the intensity of the full reveal has begun to wane, you can settle deeper into your new reality. Indulge yourself and enjoy. As the Moon has moved through waxing to waning, this is the beginning of a less active and more receptive phase. This means that you can simply sit with the ebbing fullness of what is. Begin a process of compassionate review. What have you learned? What will you do differently in the next Moon cycle? Each lunar cycle reveals an older, more experienced version of who you are becoming. So sink into this moment of reflection and get to know yourself once more.

Obsidian offers a protective energy that buffers and supports. Use it at the Waning Gibbous phase of the Moon cycle to release the past and securely recline into the experience of the moment. Obsidian's cleansing vibes can help you remove any junk from your thought patterns, allowing you to think from a new perspective. Harness its clarifying energy to appraise your situation with equanimity and objectivity.

Tiger's Eye is for encouragement and strength as you review your progress and make plans for improvement.

Citrine offers joy and optimism so that you can look at your accomplishments through a positive lens.

Celestite provides tranquillity as you come down off the high of the Full Moon.

PROTECTION,
STRENGTH, JOY AND
TRANQUILLITY

Waning Gibbous Moon Ritual

Pour yourself some tea, water, or other drink of your choice, and take the time to sit and quietly appreciate the moment. With your chosen crystal nearby, review your intention and gratitude lists.

LET GO

Get comfortable letting go so that you can make space for new things. At the Last Quarter Moon allow the leaves to fall and the fading plants to return to the soil. A tree drops its leaves to conserve resources. Take stock of what you want to let go of, so that you can use your energy wisely. Is there someone you need to forgive? Do you need to release your expectations and accept something about your life? Release the past or an outdated way of thinking, let go and forgive. Maybe you declutter your closet, acknowledge your reality, admit your mistakes, get really honest with yourself, or forgive yourself or others. The Last Quarter Moon asks that you put in a little effort to let go of the emotions and ideas that are taking up excess energy.

LOVE, SUPPORT,
GROUNDING AND GENTLE
SELF-REFLECTION

Rose Quartz is an emotional balm that can help you forgive yourself and others. As the Last Quarter Moon inspires you to release your expectations and accept your current reality, you need a soothing support that helps you open up compassionately. Rose Quartz brings playful, loving vibes and helps you gently accept a situation and move forward.

Rutilated Quartz offers a powerful support in following through on your intentions as you review what you've learned and plan for the next phase.

Smoky Quartz provides grounding, protection and assistance in clearing the thoughts and feelings that you are ready to release.

Amethyst is for gently releasing old mental patterns and contemplating new possibilities.

Last Quarter Moon Ritual

Create a peaceful environment and run a bath for yourself. Place a water-safe, non-toxic crystal (such as Quartz or Amethyst) in the bath while you review your intentions from this moon cycle. Repeat these affirmations, 'I make space for clarity' and 'I release the past'.

WANING CRESCENT

STILLNESS AND REST

The lunar energy is encouraging you
to turn inwards and be still. All is quiet
in the winter of your metaphorical
garden. Embracing stillness offers
many benefits. By allowing your inner
landscape to exist without judgement,
you honour who you are now. Slowing
down can also help you uncover your
values and emotional truth – which
may not be so apparent when you are
busily running around. And last but
not least, rest and quiet will help you
recharge your energy for the next cycle.
Challenge yourself to slow down and be
present in the moment. There will be
ample time for new plans and dreams
when the next cycle begins.

Serpentine can help you open a
gateway to the stillness within and
to the profound interconnectedness
of the universe. Using this crystal
during your Waning Crescent Moon
meditations will help you feel buffered
and supported in the understanding
that there is no-one you need to be and
nothing you need to do. Float along
with the waves of existence. You'll know
when the time is right again for action.

Selenite radiates cleansing energy that
can help you release the past cycle and
prepare to make a fresh start.

Howlite soothes your spirit and
quietens any absurd complaints from
your 'inner critic'.

Aquamarine helps you create a
meditative state of mind so that you can
listen to the stillness within.

CONNECTION WITH
NATURE, CLEANSING,
SOOTHING AND REFLECTION

Waning Crescent Moon Ritual

Sit quietly in the meditation of your choosing. Hold your
crystal or place it nearby.

MERCURY
RETROGRADE

Mercury Retrograde deserves attention as it's a chance to review your plans and goals. It's notoriously known for causing technology and communication issues, but the upside of this time period is that it offers an invitation to slow down and re-assess where you are and where you want to go.

Fast-moving Mercury symbolizes connection, communication and technology. Mercury is the part of you that learns, thinks, teaches and talks.

Mercury orbits the Sun about four times as fast as the Earth and every time that Mercury zips past the Earth an optical illusion occurs that makes it look as though Mercury is moving backwards. When Mercury appears to be moving backwards (Mercury Retrograde), it's a great opportunity to slow down. Go back over your thoughts and decisions of recent months and review them. Turn inwards to gain guidance from your intuition.

Mercury Retrograde happens about three times a year and lasts for about three weeks each time. You can use these retrograde periods as a moment to check in with yourself and review your practices, thoughts and relationships. Have you been putting off an uncomfortable conversation? Is there something that you need to be honest about with yourself when it comes to relationships, work or money? What has your body been trying to tell you? Is there some new way that you could step out of your comfort zone? What would help you feel more secure and supported?

Underlying issues tend to rise to the surface during Mercury Retrograde. It's typically advised to make sure that you are extra clear in your communications during these periods, and that you wait until the retrograde period has ended before beginning new projects or signing contracts. But it's an excellent time to pick up where you left off on something – to rethink, redo and review.

YOUR CRYSTAL PRACTICE DURING MERCURY RETROGRADE

Crystal energy can help you slow down your busy mind and tune into your intuition during Mercury Retrograde. As you rethink and review, these crystals will amplify your intuition and clarity.

KEEN INSIGHT

Pietersite Employ this speckled Quartz for illuminated insight paired with steady determination.

CREATIVE THOUGHT

Citrine A crystal that spurs your imagination, helping you conceptualize how you might like patterns or situations to change.

CLARITY AND COMMUNICATION

Aquamarine This stone soothes and calms the mind while simultaneously boosting your ability to communicate clearly.

Beginning of Mercury Retrograde Ritual

Perform a full and gentle review of the issues most affecting you by writing a journal entry using the following prompt: 'What do I need to see that I'm not seeing when it comes to my …' Give yourself lots of gratitude in the process and call on your chosen crystal to provide understanding and clarity. When you've finished, write down three takeaways on a small piece of paper and place your crystal on top of it for the remainder of the Retrograde. Drawing on the power of your crystal, let your subconscious mind continue to explore and reveal the subtleties of these thoughts and questions over the coming weeks.

End of Mercury Retrograde Ritual

Near the end of the Retrograde cycle, set an intention to integrate what you've learned during the past days and weeks. Begin by returning to your piece of paper and your crystal. What came up for you during Mercury Retrograde? Was there a new realization, attitude or interest that emerged? Think about what you may have realized and journal about what you'd like to bring into your life now. Is there an intention (see page 22) or affirmation that could come from this exploration? If so, write it down. Look in a mirror and repeat your intention or affirmation five times while holding your crystal. Remember to thank your crystal and to thank yourself for showing up. For the next two weeks, repeat this daily ritual.

CONCLUSION

This book has taken you deep below the Earth's surface, through the metaphorical caverns of crystals and their symbolism. You've connected the dots of the solar system and the meaning of the astrology you were born with. By pairing the forces of the stars above with the crystals below, you've gained tools that can help you navigate your unique journey with wisdom.

In Part Two, you learned about the crystals that can support your unique astrology. This section included insights for Virgo Sun, Moon and Rising signs, along with supportive crystal recommendations for what your sign needs in five key life areas.

Life is always changing and so in Part Three you learned to follow the energy of the Sun as it moves on its annual journey through the zodiac, finding crystals that may help you elaborate on the theme of each astrological season.

Revolving and evolving with changing astrological cycles continued in Part Four, where you paired crystal energy with the ebb and flow of the Moon, and learned to harness the power of crystals in tandem with Mercury Retrograde to perform a trimonthly check-in.

All the answers are already within you. When you choose a crystal, you awaken the vibration of that crystal within yourself. Harness your astro-crystal practice to help you see what already exists inside of you. You have everything you need.

With the cosmos above and the crystals below, you are always connected and supported. Let the stones and the stars strengthen your self-awareness and self-trust as you continue your crystalline cosmic journey.

Crystals and astrology are not intended to be a substitute for medical advice, diagnosis or treatment. Always seek the advice of your qualified healthcare provider.

RESOURCES

GET YOUR BIRTH CHART	www.sandysitron.com/crystals
ASTROLOGY READING	www.sandysitron.com
CRYSTALS	***101 Power Crystals:*** *The Ultimate Guide to Magical Crystals, Gems, and Stones for Healing and Transformation* Judy Hall
CRYSTAL ENERGY HEALING	https://www.kalisaaugustine.com/
SOURCING CRYSTALS RESPONSIBLY	moonrisecrystals.com/
SPIRAL CRYSTALS	spiralcrystals.com/
HOOF AND PAW	hoofandpawuk.com/
ASTROLOGY	***Astrology for Yourself*** Demetra George and Douglas Bloch
AFFIRMATION WORK	Transformational coach Dana Balicki: https://danabalicki.com/
AFFIRMATION WORK	***Empowerment:*** *The Art of Creating Your Life as You Want It* Gail Straub and David Gershon
ASTROLOGY EDUCATION	www.thestrology.com
	Ritual Enchantments: *A Modern Witch's Guide to Self-Possession* Mya Spalter

LAURENCE KING

First published in Great Britain in 2022 by Laurence King
an imprint of The Orion Publishing Group Ltd
Carmelite House, 50 Victoria Embankment
London EC4Y 0DZ

An Hachette UK Company

10 9 8 7 6 5 4 3 2 1

A CIP catalogue record for this book is
available from the British Library.

ISBN 978-0-8578-2933-7

Design: Therese Vandling

Printed in China by C&C Offset Printing Co. Ltd

Laurence King Publishing is committed to ethical and
sustainable production. We are proud participants in the
Book Chain Project®. [bookchainproject.com]

BOOK
CHAIN
PROJECT

www.laurenceking.com
www.orionbooks.co.uk

FEATURED CRYSTALS